CHIEF JAY STRONGBOW IS REAL
POEMS BY TIMOTHY GAGER

ISBN: 978-1-945917-18-9

Printed in the United States of America

Cover Design: Timothy Gager and Christopher Reilley

Also by Timothy Gager:

Grand Slams: A Coming of Eggs Story
The Thursday Appointments of Bill Sloan
The Shutting Door
Treating A Sick Animal: Flash and Micro Fictions

T | BIG TABLE Publishing

"Making other books jealous since 2004"

Big Table Publishing Company
Boston, MA
www.bigtablepublishing.com

To those who fought and are still fighting the battle to make this world a kinder place. Also, to those who think about love rather than advancement and who would like the quote below from Marcus Aurelius to be reality for all…

"When you arise in the morning, think of what a precious privilege it is to be alive — to breathe, to think, to enjoy, to love."
~Marcus Aurelius-

With love to
Gabe, Caroline, Teisha, Robin, Rusty, Peg, Charlie, Martha,
Mary, Fred, Bill W., and Dr. Bob

Table of Contents

PREFACE

When I was in the sixth grade, I was assigned to create a rendition of The Trail of Tears—the forced removals of Native American nations from their ancestral homelands in the Southeastern United States to an area west of the Mississippi River that had been designated as Native Territory. I collected a box, some sand from Long Beach, glue, and balled-up newspaper. At the St. James Five and Dime I bought some fierce-looking plastic "Indian" figures and a covered wagon, and with the plastic brush-looking things from my Fort Comanche play set, I was ready to roll.

My mother had an art degree from Pratt University, and with her help, the diorama portrayed a lineup of figurines and the covered wagon, trekking across hills of sand. Sounds like an A, doesn't it?

The grade I received wasn't an A. To my recollection, it was an F. The reason? My teacher thought that the five and dime Indians, whooping with axes and ready for battle, were not depicting the overwhelming sadness of these displaced individuals. I was outraged at the unfairness; the Five and Dime didn't sell figures that were crying and grieving!

But my teacher's comments stuck with me, and made me aware of this country's depiction of Native Americans. There's Chief Knock-a-Homer for the Atlanta Braves, Chief Wahoo for the Cleveland Indians, and of course, the emblem on the helmets of the Washington Redskins. In the sixties and early seventies, there was a professional wrestler, Chief Jay Strongbow (played by an Italian wrestler named Joe Scarpa,) who would go on the "warpath" and defeat his opponents to the cheers of rabid fans in packed arenas. The matches would always be the same: Strongbow would start well, almost pinning his opponent, then the opponent would rally and really hurt Jay. The injured and often crying Jay would then begin a low energy war dance, and slowly gain more and more power as he took over the match; his dancing more vigorous, his punches more deadly, until finally he won. Jay Strongbow was arguably the biggest racist gimmick in history.

Fast forward to 2017. We are still taking land from the Native Americans at Standing Rock. We still depict those of "featured" ethnic groups as people to fear, and enact travel bans against all within that group. We have overwhelming police action, force, and incarceration in higher percentages from those disempowered. We have leadership treating addictions as personal weakness rather than disease. Things are viewed as true or real because society is telling us they are true and real. In other words, if we are not advancing in all these thought patterns, we have been regressing.

I realize I do not have the direct experience to be within these sociological and political patterns. What I can do is write about them, as an outsider looking in, because as the media becomes more and more directed to report what should be reported, I as a writer have not yet been censored. I, and hopefully we as human entities, will continue to speak up without being squashed when wrongdoings are noticed. We will not do so because of narrow agendas or for ratings but rather, because what we believe in is the right thing for us all. May we continue to hold and recognize these truths as self-evident. I hope you remember how the rest of that phrase ends.

Timothy Gager, May, 2017
Boston, MA

Act I

The Part of The Chief Will Be Played by an Italian

Chief Jay Strongbow is Real

His war dance began when wounded,
Desperate, he'd rally—proud warrior

The show is real, dammit, the native American
will make that comeback, always fighting

harder when down, then full of fist-chops,
he'd punch, Handsome Jimmy Valiant

the rival's white hair was bloody and disheveled—
Valiant was formerly a partner, as champions

They fought Mr. Fugi and Professor Toru Tanaka
a tag-team battle of racism. The bout was over

when we enacted The Indian Removal Act
colonial conflict, disease, discrimination

because that was too real, dammit—the money
is what it's about. Value

Last year at Standing Rock, Junior
Wrestler Delany Lester won

the 152-pound class in a pin.
No one will remember Delany

And who was Luke Joseph Scarpa?
He was a fake, an actor within

the theater of our absurdity. It's all fake
Chief Jay Strongbow will beat the white man.

Throw Certainty Out in the Air like a Lasso
Reflections on Alton Sterling

Hatred is a deafening siren
warnings of a terrible twister

out there, it's only one. Earth
tilled by a machine We need topsoil,

moisture, fertilizer to grow a single weed
left bent. Throw questions out in the air

like a lasso. Shady, when the closed rope
loosened, it's what we know of the truth.

Repatriation

For the Kennewick Man

They've taken your bones
from nine thousand years;

don't worry The Smithsonian
says, it's unrelated to you

you are the example—the most
complete skeleton of a person

you are no longer the air,
no longer the wind, the land

no longer a mountain
built by a coyote

your people believed in
that parable with the Grizzly

stories important how you all belonged
in this place, where they take one thing

or many anothers from your history
not worth its value in customs

They'll take the water, the land,
the air if they could, so they lie

about worth and steal from the truth
that you're related to them

It's still happening, now, as
science, debunked their tall tale

that I wasn't really a native American,
not a cultural item of lineal descendants

see what they dug up, check the DNA
which shows, I still long to be in the ground.

Methinks We Protest

For Hanna Arendt, Malcolm X, Stalin and Shakespeare

And Wake up
To the same day
Protest the same day

The most radical revolutions
Become conservative
The day after the revolution

Take that out of your vocabulary
If you're not ready to perish
For expression, you must perish

So you must say, fuck you motherfucker
Confident so it won't burn your lips
Mother country cannot kiss those lips

And We cannot do this
With silk gloves
Or insulated waterproof ski gloves

Make things warm and the peaceful
Possible, so that protests
Feel real, we really doth protest

Much to do about marching
and lighting candles
marching, and lighting candles

Complacent heroes seized by pepper spray
wilting like diurnal animals at night
Feel the darkness. Feel the opposite of light.

And Wake up
To the same day
Protest the same day

Making American History

Too bad it is what it is
nothing about what it isn't.

Us, hiding from facts, sense
compassion. Humans

can be the worst thing we have.
cashing in on society's sell out

And so is war,
and so is takeover,

and so is health care
and so is prison

and so is this,
so is that

the way we write history. Nationalist slant?
It's drilled into us, Damn straight

a great sellout, a fracking disaster
Sometimes we cheat our landowners

From their ownership—money
For perdition, the cash is too good

right in our backyard, sign the contracts
then set the tap water on fire,

careful, you might blow it
(note to our forefathers)

we still wave the flag with our arms
bearing the fatigue of depletion.

I'm Feeling Good About Amerika

After Gerald Ford's campaign song

Take Sominex tonight and sleep
after Coke and a smile
is how you spell relief

The ancient Chinese secret
sauce—East meets West
we swing American

Bistro, burger, baby back
Baby back, baby back
Chili's back to the can

This is HorMel's
Diner, Kiss my grits
Quaker's testimony

Or Ford's 1976 model Gerald,
The most precious gift of all
We are at peace—

Didn't See it Before I Stepped in it

After my Dodge sat in flood water,
After it miraculously started,
After the floorboard dried,
The car still smelled of the dog turd
I'd stepped in last November.

After I drenched it with Fabreze
After I sprayed OdorGone
After I sneezed for days
After it all
after the afters.

After the excuses After all votes
I pretend, this presidency
is kind of "earthy"
After the rain I am
driving this car like a boat

1984-2017

It's nighttime twenty-four hours
We can go there any time

We can watch crusaders wallow
We can get angry at anger

The circle defying logic, there's that
lie when I wanted to stop drinking

without wanting to stop, tricked
to not have accountability

now, I realize our country
thinks the same way, doesn't

Comprehend, the lies, you know,
Words have meaning, Kelly Conway,

looks like my drunken aunt,
thin skin under her eyes

like parched leather, created
by the acidity of your words

your foot is burning,
like a lover who works—

takes the money to lie, a hollow,
experience, marching until, we stop

This Old Gym

Today, the planks warped
from heat like curved

spines coiling
through the years,

no longer honest, authentic.
There used to be a bench here,

now only a mark, painted
lines no longer seen.

I used to be a gym rat here
My games ran quick until

A winner catches
virtue and decency

now only the buzzer goes off.
most things endlessly broken

Act II
What Doesn't Kill You

But you forgot, to remember

It rains cats and dogs
and images of baby animals
made the blues go away

Billie Holiday scratched
to the end, the needle dragged
never piercing her center, which

was glued on, nevertheless,
I related. Her story intrigued,
I never understood the song's

connotation, why the singer's depths
of despair, strung me along with
desperate notes, desperate measures.

Lady—you once spoke to me,
but never knew me, all the times
I slipped this record into the sleeve

My Name is Paul

After Trouble Boys

Sylvia Plath made the pillows
and I've grown up, forever
too late and pill-popping.

Here I go, passing out over
an oven door. It's better
to contemplate getting off

the sofa, being proficient
at making my basement public
instead of sequestering there—why

not the kitchen, where everyone hangs
wrecked loose, not never drinking, certainly
I know why, how I have kept brave;

today, there's a four-year old boy
still hiding, if someone comes seeking,
I'm here, but they can't see me.

A Request

What doesn't kill you makes you thinner
Disappearing angel, life's a wish
stuck on God I wish life was better

Not what you pray for—better pray
for patience, for healing, for existence
a gun barrel aims at you, avoid it,

receive strength
never pull a trigger
cry out my name

By the Fifth Drink on Sunday Afternoon

I am aware of plastic
Peeling off the placemats

you, my spouse
the dark husband,

I, sun-drenched;
say, pass the salt

dear, with emphasis,
on your permission

obviously fumed
dinner steams

from his open mouth,
like a steam engine surging;

By the sixth, I notice this tastes raw
as he remarked about his work partner,

No one will ever know
was only a lie he gave

everyone a job chewing
stiffly at existence's toughness.

Enthusiastically he pushed— pulled
the sharp edge through the flesh

I've imagined him in the bedroom
carving his body into her,

then right now, he's using,
the blade to kill me.

The Night Wind

A balled-up piece of paper
windblown down a street

seen from a window
level to street lights

It looks dark if you don't sleep.
Night and love, wisdom like madness

methods shuffled in cards
ripped a tarp covering a roof

The mattress broke
in love, I stayed too

long in the game
a donkey waits for

the Queen of hearts, bent
at the corners, the crinkled

sheets choke my feet,
killed by mistakes.

A pair of geese fly strongly,
mate for life she said. Once

pain is small, fragile like
a seagull's tiny wing bone

snaps in a storm, it can be saved.
So I think.

The Filth and the Fury

I was drunk when the food disappeared,
the kitchen, I felt, remained
empty, the water—rain down my throat,
I forgot to shut off the faucet.

I was dry, barren, I still had some cheese
in my hand, the rat
bit my finger—it's your louse
just replaced by a cage.

Close your eyes, picture this:
a film, where epic moments
are left, cut on the dying room floor,
the horrendous ones played

background music over the scene,
when I threw your bag, as you packed,
something broke inside,
important stuff, which held me together

tonight, I know little birds fly nocturnally,
only I can't lift my own
un-winged future, unwritten on a broadside,
which said, "forever."

Tales Which Moved Me

I was never so stirred when surrounded
by death, you say, he, most imperative

the brother, who held the family together,
ODed plus Timmy, Stevie, Buddy shattered

the week with tiers of the departed,
I remain timeworn without comfort,

zilch—you and I filled the voids
with soft hips pushing at sadness

pinned you against a wall, smooth
perfection; the stroke of eye-shadow,

I watch your irises open faintly, the blooms
burst deep, into me, you've opened wider

Wash Away Her Sins

She lists with the passion
down the grocery aisle

Reflective Ambiences
Fabric Softener, spiritually

sound she is
in the moment

every Saturday
when the empty

basket is apostolic.
Dear God, is she is clean?

Prayer by a Stream

God, I've sat on my knees,
in the slowing brook,

brackish tributaries. I'd hoped
the muddy banks could hinder

the deluge unfolding
if only, I could drink

the years pinched tight.
Slackening, you leave me

waving at the sky,
curling into a sore spot

beneath the broken frames,
the branches sliver, providing

leaves painted, subtle ground
voices: *isn't there a better place?*

Eulogy for "Dying Suddenly"

You are a bone I broke, arm dangled in a sling
Then I felt like eating what I killed, so I did

In the morning, a cigarette tray,
Coffee with sugar, because bitter I know

is the cost of running my car straight into
a stanchion, will the repairs make me stronger?

You were slumped over in bed, lips white, I protest
I never hunted an insect with a semi-automatic

The television turned on at 3:45 a.m.
something woke me today. I knew

At Her Gravesite

Forever
grass will grow,
she cannot be
perennials blooming

the dull brown bulbs,
were what she was.
the group told me once
they saw things change;

like a sapling growing
up toward the sun,
happened slowly, remember
she kissed me goodbye.

Sobriety

It can exist
drink coffee

milk, three sugars,
stirred with a straw.

Sit on the sofa,
legs curled under

view the oil paintings
hung boats and fields

thousands of brush strokes
thousands

Hartooma

White rock
Wide right

Horse's head
sits on shaft

with a round
bit to tie me to

staying anchored
while she tiptoes

between shrubs of beach
plums brushed by smooth

calves, nude, a color
of leggings, can she be

naked wearing stockings?
A floppy hat, a striped towel

thin legs as fragile as the cheap
aluminum and cloth chair

she carries the bag full
steady, heavy to hold

Act III

When We Talk About Love

It's Gaga or Nothing

Nothing

But the radio plays
concussions of hope,
holding on before you die

or Hell, just marry a bad boy
so no expectations happen
except being together,

is a bad time to try
out failed experiments
such as now — this

dating is either gaga or nothing.
we're part of the divorced mass;
brain dead — unattended in bed

without partners, you can get yourself
off the mattress — quietly sliding out of
the cold gathering of information.

The facts are: Your secret is safe with me
the same way a storm has the tendency
to wash and blow away flawless attractions.

Gaga

Two brains
making music
a must to bond.

Loving how literal you are
also being acute figurative
How's that for a dare?

But a crush is like
nervous anticipatory craving
that essential soulmate.

Intimacy — is the easy part.
The difficult — connecting
when time passes....

If a man is indifferent
in three months, he
may just be comfortable

with you, like a worn t-shirt
is a perfect imperfection.
Is a secret we told each other.

About Making Love

Something released, birds
flew homeward, better than
pigeons homing, better than
cages, we talked about
vexing inward, in land
there is dark
lit tunnels, shadowy, deep,
we talked about
making love, comfort,
and about birds.

When We Talk About Love

We talk about the wrong things
We think about the other

young girls we danced with,
They must be desperate

Let me sell it to you
Sell you something of yours

There's 13 steps you took
Then became lukewarm

the best kind of love, isn't regular
it is with a cleaning lady, a mailman

Want to see something?
It's how you kill the slugs

It's how you plan to fly away
into a negligent nonexistent role

In the future, you will go home
to take a bath, we're all unconscious

unhappy enough to smash rocks
over the heads of unwilling lovers

or denim wearing cheaters at a bingo parlor.
Did you clap when she cried out victorious?

Did you drink whiskey and keep fishing
when the body of a girl washed ashore?

A dummy near the water, built
an electric fence to keep out thoughts

My darling

my porcupine, my skunk,
my duly, in the whole wide

gopher, my animals
my mulligan, my misanthropic

curmudgeon. Kick a dog
when he's out, he's down

How We Exist

The confrontation
between water and blacktop
is elegant, how we exist,
like wash and refuse,
down a street splashed clean.
Our lives flush us out,
the hush unleashed
faintly out to sea....

In the end, it's pouring,
not letting up, please
let me compose myself
quick, it's just that
the sound of the thrashing,
by rain into my core
is a muse in the flood.
By no means stop.

Loose Flowers

You know you slay me
so what?

I have dragon breath
which once wilted lilies

when you stuck your
flowers into my mouth

At 2 AM, you say
It's never too late:

Blossoms at a cemetery
are donated to my girl

You know that smell?
you worked at a funeral home.

Your apartment housed
rooms of splendor

Whenever I stayed over I walked back
such a way, such a dead man.

Act IV
Lodged in an Airway

Counter Act

An empty bottle of wine
A suitcase never unpacked

Call for you
Every night
Like clockwork
We don't talk

We tic
We don't sleep
We knock
Self-help like an old woman's

gums worn away enough
those dentures will never fit
eye-teeth, molars, incisors
I've gnawed a lot of rock
In the cavity of cold—
The room has mosquito netting

Paler Nymph

See the eyes get shoddier
faded green, gray, brown
Aiming at impulsiveness

The Sylph is graceful and grateful
but fork tongued, fork tailed seadogs
characterizations fail—are false

paled and cut with bleach, water
disinfects the deeper wounds
extends the life of cut flowers

deeper wounds undefended,
you'll do anything for others'
happiness, what do they think?

Ingestion

I pulled your knit winter warrior
warrior hat off with my teeth

tugged until it softly
lodged into my airway.

This suffocation leaving me
Waving like a slow fellow

needing help. Notice the blue
entering the softness of my lips

shoving your hands over,
feeling my lungs collapse

I chewed thick lead pencils
in First Grade, until they were

bumpy, strange, you tasted
the dirt under the swing-set.

This is where I Am (when here)

after your leaving, the Hungry Man was
pulled out of the microwave, telling me
you won't ever come back, you gave

a homeless man ten dollars once,
to make his eyes glimmer
but when I walked passed

today I identified and wished
him well, I meant no harm, no foul
odor, no one remembers, how I sent

bad advice, if you have a migraine,
use a pistol or a baseball bat, I lie
in this bed, this cold vacant head

wonders about empty, hallow, homes;
times when they were not that bad,
yet, I just can't help I'm at this place.

Stratus

pulling central south
beads of sweat—
a goosebump
on the car's hood

riding to reclamation
there is something higher
I own my part no worse,
no better, when life pours

problems, like a waterfall
I can't swim, hoodwinked
no more, driving
away from storm clouds.

Upon Leaving

We can split peas into little bites
feed the fish, walk on the grass

we all cry for approval, acceptance
is shelter, we take risks, we love

people who don't love us
hide it in context, we go the

separate ways we lie
on a bed of nails all set.

I shalt not want a hammer
to cut my food. Accept the truth

like a sharp wind, the cold razor rain
in your face, finally opens up

Remember the shark tank?
I swam with the blood dripping in.

I am no longer your anything

I am no longer 66 million years ago
no longer a chicken from hell, I am

left from Cretaceous–Tertiary but
let's go back, no, longer than that

when I discovered something
new then sat in the ash, fossilized

after you moved on, leaving
my burning corner of the world.

I no longer have 60 thick, conical,
bone-crunching teeth, powerful legs,

short pint-sized arms. I reached,
I ate. The world became halved.

A Shining night

Windstorm to a clothesline
Your silk nightgown
belled into a metallic sail
blowing untethered You left

the window open. Heard cars
drag racing to obvious conclusions
ending when the power line snapped
the light to darkness, to pitch black

she screamed she's leaving
she won't come back
into this nightmare—she's not
coming back into that song either

The Last Time

We'll not pretend when this moment ends
how light twists in your hair, my finger

brushes your stubborn nipple, which wishes me
no sleep, defined now as lovers still, I drift

on top, roll my head down
tired resting on your thigh, it's time

to wake-up dammit, wake-up damn…
we only tried this.

How Elephants Love

We didn't take love, forget love, we didn't
forget laughing: there's that footprint crushed

in the cheesecake again. I love you peanut,
how quaint is a touch you'll always remember.

The tusk, you stampeded into, we two Elephants
tussling the world. One night, you packed

your trunk, curled inside me in contradiction
of the hoof sunk into my open mouth.   Always

remember our grand entrance, I led you downtown,
ecstatic to be parading. You'd never run roughshod

until misunderstandings caused fatal consequences.
Remember dear Elephant, joy, anger, grief, *love*

all reside within you. Remember when
I went into musth, and you in oestrus

Reminisce how we love, isn't only that.
Remember to not forget the concept forever.

suicide sequential

sensuous brute.
bully-brained blessed scream.
backseat broadsided butt
banging, monsterpeace,
my lover, my lover, my lover.

cling to me—cadent stenographer,
whose skill soils me shadowy
lights flicking off to places
you—my *my*,
my marvel.

moon when it's dusky.
the panic button. struck me
—stagnant and sinking
walls, lie down, beg,
roll over, play dead.

Act V
Worn Away in Circulation

A Poem For Forever

this light touches like one from a fireplace
sits in the sky too, an orange sunset
paints the far edge of the world

limitlessness He'll take you
never without permission—
        you know God

create Him
a sweeping gate of untainted joy,
You made eternity, knowledge

        Love,
the transmission, You are
        All

Family, friends
chant it, think it, are
It, resending faith

symbiotic—ecstasy
not of this world.
You no longer wait

        Just receive;
        be.

Unfit Father

My children made me lose my head,
today at the beach, my patience

vanished like waves taking turns,
retracting back to the ocean.

I'm tied to their hindrance,
never to sail, never to watch,

never going back from whence
I came. A few times I wanted

to tell them why I packed
my belongings and left.

Instead I babbled about salt
percentages in their veins,

in their sweat, in their tears,
wail "we want ice-cream,"

please, pick up this faded day.
They're too young for a lesson:

Things end, things vanish, you're
frustrated with the sluggish pace.

Get on my shoulders, piggy-back,
I'll fold your sister under my arm,

a clean towel dampened with shadows,
shielded so they can't see my skull

when it shatters in certainty,
the sea rising up to empty sockets.

When I Think of my Childhood

I think of family, a picture
we hold together perhaps
a painting, the one of fruit

in a bowl. Sometimes when I stare,
I swear I see the soft parts turn
bad, the bruises. On the playground

every apparatus brought fearful results
The jungle gym, my throat choked at a bar
a see-saw comrades leapt off I sat at the top
of a slide, punched all the way to the bottom

At age sixteen, a hundred forty pounds
an empty pit, my ribs stuck out like a step ladder
my toothpick arms with bulbous hinges
I think it impossible to fill my stomach
not that we were wanting, just a never ending

well… To think was I saved by my
great escapes? I had to come back from
those years later when the Merry-go-round spun
me dry, I woke up late that morning,
still no longer a boy subsisting

living in my head was easy to do, with nothing
to do—the smoke you see raging from my ears
is just my image in the mirror, made quite a sight
of myself. I hoped to be different

Cross Country Family Vacation

Colorado was spinning
I was seven years old
Family drove across country
By Minnesota we were toast
Dad started fining us nickels
for being belligerent

Never gave up Indian heads
before Four Corners
merging to a point
My mother took a picture
Us being miserable—sister crying
My dad feigning a laugh

Act VI
God, We Need Such *Luxury*

Found on Social Media

Cow tries prosthetic leg for the first time
This made me weep
Can I have an amen

featuring a can of Goya black beans
I will be the keynote speaker, I'm all IN
belittling trigger warnings

comparing modern young people
with soldiers on D-Day, a whole raft
of new rules where you can be sued

following loud noises, sudden movements,
crowds of people touching you
Violence is all these thugs understand

a hit causing no devastation
what the circles of hell look like
Stay home.
Save a bird.
Read a book.
Cook a meal.
Plant a garden.

Us Defined

Per Urban Dictionary: You:
"A warm wonderful woman

People open up to her,
their bare bones visible

She can rest between ribs.
You avert winter..."

Me: *"A person with a high*
degree of confidence, maybe

because he is too skinny.
You will be surprised

how fast he moves, his swift
motions are crazy—" You and I

both know I wrote your
definition, finally, I wrote love.

Nursery Rhythms

for Mike Megna

I am a cripple, "codi-filled"
I saw the world
Through mud colored
spectacles—keep my
crooked thoughts

as a fly crows, rippled

off my crooked clavicle
sapiens discern vertebrae
unbreakable, resilient
missiled. And shatterproof
glass in pitched little houses
is how we wind up a catapult.

My Claim

That's my car
without a wheel

Ran off the road
stripped and totaled

Left me in Newton
you said never

Get rid of that one
smashed around a bend

I lied about an oncoming
vehicle that wasn't there

Just trying to please
my officer. Deductible?

Charge it to my AMEX
You know, the free miles

I'm sorry I couldn't collect
the body, the calico

In the backseat
She had a name

Making Spring Come Early

Ice scorching sonnets
temperature boasting ballads
Odes to oven like
cinquain calidity

peel off layers of clothes
the warmth of Neruda
God we need
such luxury

ACT VII
Seasoning

Hot Biscuits, Country Ham at the Loveless Motel

Lumpy gravy is what you can get, scratch
mattress, adorned with three thin blue stripes.

I could send a postcard,
wishing you here—

though you've driven on, past this room
with black mold on the shower stall

a Radio Shack clock radio.
Remember from your teens?

You: rolling onto that first love, how fresh,
almost floral scented, you hungered for

now, biscuits and country ham. A sign flashes
red through worn cloth drapes tells you so

Grumpy reply to the grumpy cashier
at the fast food restaurant
after immaturity

Hello Sunshine!
Just make my day
a damn sandwich.
That's what I'm here for

Just a reminder:
no one died on a cross
making that bun
the body of *Jesus Christ*

I'm not checking you out
when I set my eyes
on your sour puss, please
smile, say thank-you

That's your line, not mine
And salt-pepper-ketchup,
Please, go the hell home
is not my line, it's yours.

Leftovers at the Lays Potato Chip Factory

They stood half a room away;
He station A7, she at D1
picking out burnt rejects.

Her last man collected red flags
in women like challenges,
"don't tell me about me,
let's look at yourself," he said.

A conveyer belt away;
she looks up to him, a bad one
shifts through from above

a blue note mini hearts bounces
toward her, jockeying with
the Lays…she reaches for
a mistake
a miracle.

There's a Fly in My Soup

Waitress pulls a winged
Insect out from

Wonton Soup
Shifts it between

Pinching fingers
Working as a grinder

Producing blackened ash
Says, "Not fly…seasoning."

Act VIII
Survival

For the Bear

before the Revolt

Irate the green leaf
turns brown; spins, falls

in the air, shriveled, and propelled
away from home—hello,

courage. You are here now,
we will honor your furious storm

wrestling beneath the surface, hear
the wind and We cannot fear, not be moved

from water and land-please stand with us,
weary from carrying—fear you

cannot make the journey, cannot be moved
to and from the great foraging fields to feed

The plant will speak of sacrifice,
so shoot first—obligate existence.

Some of the poems in *Chief Jay Strongbow is Real* have
appeared in the following journals:

Taos Journal of International Poetry and Art
Ibbetson 36,38,39,40
Contemporary American Voices
Oddball Magazine
Muddy River Poetry Review
Mass Poetry Website, Poem of the Moment
Cape Cod Poetry Review, Winter 2014

www.ingramcontent.com/pod-product-compliance
Lightning Source LLC
LaVergne TN
LVHW041304080426
835510LV00009B/863